DOMINOES

The Skateboarder

QUICK STARTER 250 HEADWORDS

OXFORD
UNIVERSITY PRESS

Great Clarendon Street, Oxford, OX2 6DP, United Kingdom

Oxford University Press is a department of the University of Oxford.
It furthers the University's objective of excellence in research, scholarship, and education by publishing worldwide. Oxford is a registered trade mark of Oxford University Press in the UK and in certain other countries

First published in Dominoes 2012
2020
17

ISBN: 978 0 19 424946 1 Book
ISBN: 978 0 19 463908 8 Book and Audio Pack

Printed in China

This book is printed on paper from certified and well-managed sources

ACKNOWLEDGEMENTS

Illustrations by: Pete Smith/Beehive Illustration Agency

The publisher would like to thank the following for permission to reproduce photographs: Getty Images p.23 (woman skateboarding/Stan Liu/Iconica).

Cover photo: Corbis (detail of young boy standing on skateboard/beyond).

DOMINOES

Series Editors: Bill Bowler and Sue Parminter

The Skateboarder

Christine Lindop

Illustrated by Pete Smith

Christine Lindop was born in New Zealand and taught English in France and Spain before settling in Great Britain. She has written or adapted more than thirty books, including *The Turn of the Screw* and *Green Planet* in the Dominoes series. In her free time she likes reading, watching films, and making mosaic. She is not a skateboarder, but she likes watching the action at her local skatepark, and her favourite sports are rugby and Formula One.

OXFORD
UNIVERSITY PRESS

Story Characters

Hannah

Justin

Owen

Hannah's mother

Hannah's father

Evan

Michael

Michael's mother

A woman in the street

Contents

Before Reading ... vi

Chapter 1 **No skateboard** ... 1

Activities ... 3

Chapter 2 **Good grades, better presents** ... 4

Activities ... 7

Chapter 3 **First steps** ... 8

Activities ... 11

Chapter 4 **Practice, practice, practice** ... 12

Activities ... 15

Chapter 5 **Up early** ... 16

Activities ... 19

Chapter 6 **A real skateboarder** ... 20

Activities ... 23

Project A ... 24

Project B ... 26

Word Work ... 28

Grammar ... 31

About Dominoes ... 34

ACTIVITIES

BEFORE READING

1 Hannah wants to be a skateboarder. In the story, all of these people help her. What do they do?

Hannah's mother and father

Owen

A woman in the street

Justin

Michael

Evan

Match these sentences with the pictures and write the names.

a .... He helps her to skateboard better.
b .... He gives her a helmet for her head.
c .... He goes to the skatepark with her.
d .... They give a skateboard to her.
e .... Hannah changes after she watches him.
f .... She smiles at Hannah and says, 'Don't stop.'

2 In this story, two people learn to do new things. Who are they? What do they learn to do?

Person	Learns to …

Chapter 1 – No skateboard

Near Hannah's house there's a new **skatepark**. A lot of young people in the town go there after **school** with their **skateboards**.

These days Hannah often goes there with her **cousin** Justin. Justin goes to school with her. Hannah doesn't like school very much, or getting up early. She's always late. And she doesn't have many friends. But with the new skatepark, she's suddenly very interested in skateboarding. The only thing is – Hannah has no skateboard!

skatepark a place where people can skateboard

school students learn here

skateboard a board with little wheels that can move fast; to go on a skateboard

cousin the son (or daughter) of your mother's (or father's) sister (or brother)

Sometimes Justin asks Hannah, 'Hey, do you want to get on my skateboard?' So she does – but not for long. She doesn't want to **fall off** in front of everybody. So usually she watches the skateboarders.

Owen is fifteen. He's a good skateboarder. He can do a lot of **tricks**.

'I love Owen's skateboarding,' Hannah thinks. 'I want to **jump** and do tricks, too.'

'Why don't you have a skateboard, Hannah?' Justin asks her.

'It's a new thing for me – skateboarding,' Hannah answers. Then she thinks, 'My **birthday**'s coming. **Maybe** I can talk to Mom and Dad.'

fall off to go down from something suddenly

trick a clever way of moving on a skateboard

jump to move suddenly from one place to a different place; when you move suddenly from one place to a different place

birthday the day when someone is a year older

maybe perhaps

ACTIVITIES

READING CHECK

Are these sentences true or false? Tick the boxes.

	True	False
a The new skatepark is near Hannah's school.	☐	☑
b Hannah is Justin's cousin.	☐	☐
c Hannah has a lot of friends.	☐	☐
d Hannah doesn't have a skateboard.	☐	☐
e Justin doesn't have a skateboard.	☐	☐
f Hannah doesn't want to fall off.	☐	☐
g Hannah loves Owen's skateboarding.	☐	☐
h It is Justin's birthday soon.	☐	☐

GUESS WHAT

What happens in the next chapter? Tick two boxes in a, b and c.

a For her birthday, Hannah has …
- **1** ☐ a skateboard.
- **2** ☐ a school bag.
- **3** ☐ something to wear.

b Hannah's older brother Evan …
- **1** ☐ laughs at her.
- **2** ☐ gives something nice to her.
- **3** ☐ is angry with her.

c The weekend after her birthday, Hannah …
- **1** ☐ laughs at Owen.
- **2** ☐ falls off her skateboard.
- **3** ☐ leaves the skatepark.

Chapter 2 – Good grades, better presents

On Hannah's birthday morning, she opens her **presents**. There's a big present from her mother and father. Hannah opens it first, excitedly.

'Wow!' she cries. 'A skateboard! Thanks!'

'Well, your school **grades** are good, Hannah,' her mother says. 'And it *is* your birthday ... So happy birthday, **honey**!'

'Now open that present,' her father says. 'It's from Evan.' Hannah opens it. It's a **helmet**.

'**Awesome**!' Hannah cries. But her older brother, Evan, laughs.

'You like watching skateboarding videos, I know,' he

present something that you give to someone

grades the numbers or letters that teachers give to school work to show when it is good or bad

honey something that you say to someone you love

helmet a hard hat that people wear when they skateboard

awesome very good

says. 'But do you ... er ... skateboard?'

'Yes, I do,' Hannah says hotly, 'sometimes – on Justin's skateboard! And I have *my* skateboard now. So I can do more.'

'Can you jump, or do tricks?' Evan asks. 'Can you go fast and stay on?'

'Duh!' Hannah answers her brother angrily. 'What **dumb** questions!'

'Evan, honey, please,' their mother says. 'It's Hannah's birthday.'

'OK,' Evan says.

That weekend, Hannah takes her new skateboard to the skatepark with Justin. There aren't many people there. Hannah is excited.

dumb stupid

'OK! Let's go,' Justin says. The two cousins begin skateboarding. Justin does a trick. Hannah skateboards up and down.

'Maybe I can jump now,' she thinks. She goes faster. Then she jumps – but she falls off her skateboard.

When Hannah is on the **ground**, somebody laughs.

'Oh, no! They're laughing at me! This is **awful**!' she thinks. She gets up quickly.

'I'm going,' she tells Justin, and she leaves.

Just then, Owen arrives with his friends. They're laughing at a picture of Owen on his phone.

But Hannah's far away now. 'No more skateboarding for me!' she thinks.

ground we walk on this

awful very bad

ACTIVITIES

READING CHECK

Choose the correct words to complete these sentences.

a Hannah has her birthday presents in the *morning* / *evening*.

b Her school grades are *bad* / *good* now.

c The helmet is from her *mother* / *brother*.

d Hannah goes to the skatepark with *Justin* / *Owen*.

e When Hannah jumps at the skatepark, she *falls* / *laughs*.

f Hannah says, 'I'm *going* / *crying*.'

g Owen's friends are laughing at a picture of *Hannah* / *Owen*.

h Hannah *never* / *always* wants to skateboard again.

GUESS WHAT

What happens in the next chapter? Tick the boxes.

a Justin …
- **1** ☐ goes to the skatepark.
- **2** ☐ stays at home with his family.

b Hannah …
- **1** ☐ sits in the sun.
- **2** ☐ falls off her skateboard again.

c A baby boy …
- **1** ☐ is learning to walk.
- **2** ☐ is learning to speak.

Chapter 3 – First steps

The next day, Justin stays at home with his family. But Hannah walks past the skatepark. A lot of people are doing tricks.

'I can't skateboard there now,' Hannah thinks. She watches Owen on his skateboard. He goes up in the **air** and comes down again.

'He's awesome,' Hannah thinks. 'And I'm awful.'

She leaves the skatepark, and begins to walk home through the **park**.

The sun is hot. Hannah sits down on one of the park **benches**. The sun is in her eyes. So she closes them.

air the space above and around things

park a big garden that is open to everyone to visit

bench you can sit on this in a garden or park

When she opens her eyes again, she sees a young woman near her. She is sitting on the **grass** with her **baby** boy. The little boy is **trying** to stand.

'Good boy, Michael,' his mother says. 'Stand up now. Yes, that's right!'

Michael stands up slowly. He takes one little **step** and **falls down**.

'Come on, now, Michael!' his mother says. 'Don't cry. Try again.'

Michael stops crying and laughs. He takes his mother's hand, and stands up again.

'Good boy, Michael,' his mother says.

Michael sits down suddenly. He laughs, and **claps** his hands happily.

grass it is green; gardens and fields have a lot of it on the ground

baby a very young child

try to begin to do something that you can't do very well

step when you move from one foot to the other

fall down to go down suddenly onto the ground

clap to hit your hands together to show that you like something

Hannah watches them for five minutes. Michael stands up and falls down, again and again.

'Try again, Michael,' his mother says.

'He doesn't stop falling. But it doesn't matter,' Hannah thinks. 'He gets up and tries again – time after time. And he's no more than a baby.'

Hannah leaves the park and walks home. She thinks about baby Michael. 'OK,' she says, 'I need some more skateboard **practice**. But where can I go for that?'

practice when you do something many times so that you can do it well

ACTIVITIES

READING CHECK

Match the characters from Chapter 3 with the sentences.

Justin | Owen | Michael | Michael's mother | Hannah

a ....Justin.... stays at home.
b .... thinks, 'I'm awful.'
c .... goes up in the air and comes down again.
d .... is sitting on the grass with her baby.
e .... takes his mother's hand.
f .... says, 'Try again.'
g .... claps his hands.
h .... thinks about baby Michael when she walks home.
i .... needs some more skateboard practice.

GUESS WHAT

What happens in the next chapter? Tick the boxes.	**Yes**	**No**
a Hannah finds a parking lot near her house.	☐	☐
b She does skateboard practice there in the morning.	☐	☐
c She finds no cars in the parking lot when she visits it.	☐	☐
d When she first tries jumping, she falls off her skateboard.	☐	☐
e A woman on a bicycle laughs at Hannah.	☐	☐
f Some days later, Hannah jumps and doesn't fall off.	☐	☐
g That evening, Hannah tells her mother about her practice.	☐	☐
h Hannah is very happy when Evan comes in.	☐	☐

Chapter 4 – Practice, practice, practice

'Hmm. Let's see. The skatepark's no good,' Hannah thinks. 'I want to do my practice **alone**.'

That evening, she goes for a walk. Two **blocks** from her house there's an office building. At half past five, everybody in it goes home. They drive all their cars out of the **parking lot**. 'Hey, I can skateboard *here*!' Hannah thinks.

The next evening, she takes her skateboard and helmet with her.

'I'm going out for some skateboard practice,' she tells her mother.

She skateboards to the parking lot. There are no cars there. First, she skateboards slowly. She is alone, and nobody is watching.

alone with nobody

block a number of buildings together with streets all round them

parking lot people leave their cars here

'This is awesome!' she thinks. After an hour, she goes home.

She skateboards most evenings. Soon she can go fast. One evening, she tries jumping. She skateboards across the parking lot, and jumps. Suddenly, she is on the ground.

A woman is going past on a bicycle. She sees Hannah on the ground, and smiles at her.

'**Bad luck**,' she calls. 'Try again.'

So Hannah tries once more – and falls off her skateboard again. She laughs, gets up, and goes home.

Two days later, Hannah is back in the parking lot. She jumps again. This time she *doesn't* fall off.

bad luck you say this when something bad happens to somebody

At home that evening, her mother says, 'You're happy about something, honey! Tell me. What is it?'

'Well ... ,' Hannah begins, 'don't laugh, OK?'

'OK.'

'The practice is helping. I can do good skateboard jumps now. Uh ... usually.'

'That's wonderful, honey!'

Just then, Evan comes in.

'Oh, no!' Hannah thinks. 'What does he want?'

ACTIVITIES

READING CHECK

Correct the mistakes in the sentences.

a Hannah wants to do skateboard practice ~~with her friends~~ alone.

b There are no cars in the parking lot before half past five.

c Hannah walks to the parking lot.

d A woman on a skateboard smiles at Hannah.

e She says, 'Good luck' to her.

f When Hannah falls off again, she cries.

g After two days, Hannah can always do good skateboard jumps.

h Hannah is talking to her mother when Evan goes out.

GUESS WHAT

What happens in the next chapter? Tick three sentences.

a ☐ Evan doesn't talk to Hannah.

b ☐ Hannah has a lot of bruises.

c ☐ Evan skateboards at the skatepark.

d ☐ A lot of people visit the skatepark in the early morning.

e ☐ Evan helps Hannah with a good idea.

f ☐ Hannah sometimes arrives late at school.

g ☐ Hannah never thinks about baby Michael.

h ☐ Justin tells Hannah about 'Go Skateboarding Day'.

i ☐ Hannah forgets her skateboard.

Chapter 5 – Up early

'Hey! How's your new skateboard?' Evan asks Hannah nicely.

Their mother smiles at this. Then she quickly leaves the room.

'Oh, it's not bad,' Hannah answers, 'and the helmet's awesome, too. But I have a lot of **bruises** now. Look.'

Evan looks at the bruises all over her arms and legs. 'Ouch!' he says. 'So do you skateboard at the skatepark now?'

'No,' Hannah answers. 'There are always a lot of people there. But I want to go up the **walls**. I want to **turn** in the air, too.'

bruise a dark mark on your skin that comes after something hits it

wall something strong and thick that you can go up on a skateboard

turn to move round

'Well, I go past the skatepark every day when I go to work. There's nobody there in the early morning,' Evan says.

'Evan! That's an awesome **idea**!' Hannah cries. 'I can go there before school. Thanks.'

Next day, Hannah gets up at six o'clock. She skateboards for an hour before school.

'This is wonderful!' her mother says a week later. 'Hannah's up early every morning these days. She's never late for school now!'

Sometimes Hannah is tired in the morning. But then she remembers baby Michael.

'Babies get up early,' she thinks. 'So I can get up early, too.'

idea something that you think

One Saturday afternoon, her cousin Justin calls her on the phone.

'Hey, Hannah, are you coming tomorrow?

'Coming where? What's tomorrow?'

'It's June 21st – 'Go Skateboarding Day'. People all **around** the **world** are skateboarding. I'm going to the skatepark with all my friends. Come with us.'

'OK!' Hannah says. 'See you there.'

'Don't forget your skateboard,' Justin says.

'Justin, don't be dumb,' Hannah answers.

around all the way round

world people live in a lot of different countries here

ACTIVITIES

READING CHECK

Choose the correct words to complete these sentences.

a Evan asks about Hannah's *grades* / *skateboard*.
b Hannah likes her *helmet* / *bruises*.
c Hannah wants to go *up* / *over* the walls on her skateboard.
d Evan goes past the skatepark when he goes to *school* / *work*.
e Hannah gets up at *six* / *eight* o'clock.
f Sometimes Hannah is *hungry* / *tired* in the morning.
g 'Go Skateboarding Day' is on *June* / *August* 21st.
h Justin calls Hannah on the *radio* / *phone*.
i 'Don't be *dumb* / *late*,' Hannah says to Justin.

GUESS WHAT

What happens in the next chapter? Complete each sentence with the correct name.

Hannah	Justin	Michael	Owen

a .... goes to the skatepark with her skateboard.
b She sees .... there with his friends.
c .... does a tough trick.
d .... falls off his skateboard.
e .... asks, 'How do you do that trick?'
f .... says, 'You're a real skateboarder now.'
g .... walks home through the park with Hannah.
h .... walks across the grass to his mother.
i .... asks about baby Michael.

Chapter 6 – A real skateboarder

It's June 21st. Hannah finds her skateboard and helmet. Then she goes to the skatepark. She's excited.

'Can I do this?' she thinks. 'Hmmm. I don't know. But I can try!'

At the skatepark, Hannah sees Justin with some friends. She goes over to them.

'Hey, Hannah,' Justin says. 'Watch this. Owen's doing a very **tough** trick.'

Owen goes up the wall and turns. He goes very **high**. Everybody stops and watches.

'Wow!' Hannah says. 'He's awesome.'

tough not easy

high far up from the ground

Owen does a different trick now. It's an easy trick, but this time he falls off his skateboard. He walks past Hannah and smiles at her.

'Everybody falls off sometimes,' Owen says.

'**Sure**,' Hannah answers. 'How do you do that trick? I want to learn it.'

'Put your right foot here,' Owen tells her. 'Then **push** with your left foot.' Owen helps Hannah with the trick.

'OK,' Hannah says. 'I need some more practice with that, but thanks.'

'You're a **real** skateboarder now, Hannah,' Justin tells her quietly after that.

sure when you want to say 'yes' to somebody, you say this

push to move something away from you

real true

Later, Hannah and Justin walk home through the park. Hannah sees baby Michael again. He is walking across the grass to his mother. This time he doesn't take her hand, and he doesn't fall down.

'Hello,' says Hannah. She smiles at him.

'Can you do it again?' says Michael's mother. The baby laughs and claps his hands.

'Again!' he says. And he stands up.

Justin and Hannah walk away.

'Who's that?' Justin asks.

'Now? Oh, a little baby,' Hannah answers, 'but maybe one day a really good skateboarder!'

ACTIVITIES

READING CHECK

Put the sentences in order. Number them 1–10.

- **a** ☐ Owen falls down.
- **b** ☐ Hannah smiles at baby Michael.
- **c** ☐ Owen smiles at Hannah.
- **d** ☐ Hannah goes to the skatepark.
- **e** ☐ Baby Michael says, 'Again!' and stands up.
- **f** ☐ Owen helps Hannah with the trick.
- **g** ☐ Owen does a tough trick.
- **h** ☐ Hannah meets Justin.
- **i** ☐ Hannah and Justin walk home together.
- **j** ☐ Hannah finds her skateboard and helmet.

Match the first and second parts of these sentences.

a Hannah is excited	**1** with the new trick.
b She sees Justin	**2** everybody stops and watches.
c When Owen goes up the wall,	**3** when she goes to the skatepark.
d Owen's trick is easy,	**4** 'Put your right foot here.'
e Owen tells Hannah	**5** and stands up.
f Hannah needs more practice	**6** 'You're a real skateboarder now.'
g Justin says to Hannah,	**7** with some of his friends.
h Baby Michael's mother says,	**8** 'Can you do it again?'
i Michael claps his hands	**9** but he falls off his skateboard.

Project A Changes in people

1 Complete this text about Hannah with the words in the box.

a skateboard and a helmet
always late for school
doesn't have a skateboard
falls off her skateboard
grades are better
has more practice on her skateboard
sees baby Michael in the park
teaches a new trick to her

When the story begins, Hannah is **a)** . . . . She is interested in skateboarding, but she **b)** . . . . After she works harder at school, her **c)** . . . . On her birthday, she has **d)** . . . . from her mother, father, and brother.
One day at the skatepark she **e)** . . . . 'No more skateboarding for me!' she says.
The change in her happens when she **f)** . . . . He falls down, but he gets up and tries again.
Later, Hannah **g)** . . . . in a parking lot. When she falls off it, she tries again. Soon she can jump and turn.
In the end, Hannah skateboards at the skatepark with all the skateboarders. Owen **h)** . . . . She is a real skateboarder now!

2 How does Hannah's brother Evan change in the story? Use these notes to write a text about him on page 25.

When / story / begin / Evan / not be nice / to Hannah /.
He / give / present / to her, but he / ask / dumb questions /. Hannah / be angry / with him /.
The change / happen / when / mother / say / 'not be / awful to Hannah' /.
Later / Evan / ask / Hannah / about / skateboarding /.
Soon / he / be looking / at / bruises and / talking / about / skateboard practice /.
In the end / Evan / have / good idea. He / tell / sister / do / practice / in / skatepark before schoo

How do these people change in the story? Choose one of them. Write notes in the box.

Owen

Michael

Justin

When the story begins	
The change happens when	
Later	
In the end	

Write a text about your character from your notes. Use the texts in 1 and 2 to help you.

Project B An important day

1 Read this text about 'Go Skateboarding Day' and complete the table below.

'Go Skateboarding Day' happens on June 21st every year. The home of 'Go Skateboarding Day' is California, in the United States. Now you can find it in Brazil, China, France, Poland, Portugal, and many more countries.

On this day, skateboarders meet on the streets and in skateparks. Why do they come? Because they want to skateboard together. Often people watch the skateboarders and give money – for new skateparks, or for children's homes or old people's homes.

Some skateboarders wear a 'Go Skateboarding Day' T-shirt. When they are skateboarding, they meet old skateboarding friends and make new friends. All around the world, skateboarders can't wait for 'Go Skateboarding Day'!

When is 'Go Skateboarding Day'?	
Where is its home?	
In which countries can you find it now?	
Where do people meet?	
Why do they come?	
What do people often give money for on this day?	
What do some skateboarders wear?	
Who do skateboarders meet?	

Read the notes about 'World Run Day', and complete the text.

When is 'World Run Day'?	early November
Where is its home?	Long Beach, New York, the United States
In which countries can you find it now?	Afghanistan, Australia, India, UK, and more
Where do people meet?	streets, parks
Why do they come?	want to run together
What do people give money for on this day?	sick people, people without homes
What do some runners wear?	'World Run Day' T-shirt
Who do runners meet?	old running friends

'World Run Day' is in .... every year. The home of 'World Run Day' is ...., ... in the .... Now you can find it in .... and many more countries.

On this day, runners meet on .... and in .... Why do they come? Because they .... Often people watch the runners and give money – for .... or for ....

Some runners wear a .... When people are running, they can meet .... and make new ones. All around the world, runners can't wait for 'World Run Day'!

Now find out about another world day and write about it.

World Snowboard Day – December 18th

International Surfing Day – June 21st

International Dance Day – April 29th

ACTIVITIES

WORD WORK 1

1 Find words from Chapters 1 and 2 to match the pictures.

a skatepark

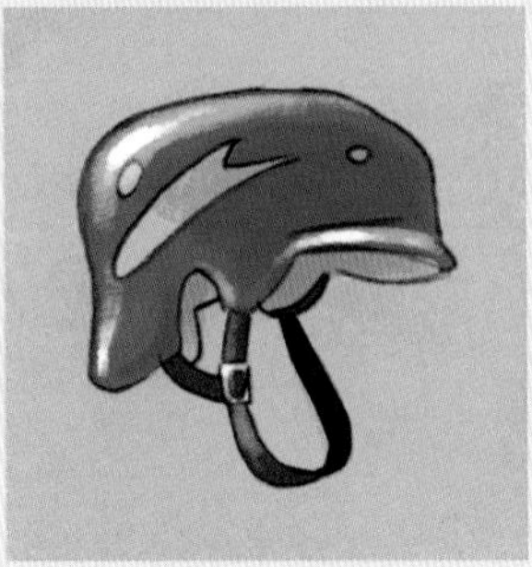

b ....

c ....

d ....

e ....

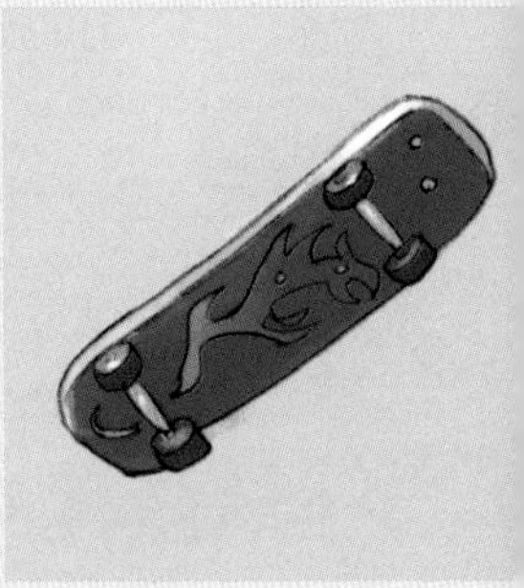

f ....

2 Match a word or phrase from the box with the underlined words in each sentence.

awesome	awful	birthday	cousin	dumb	grades	~~tricks~~

a Owen can do <u>interesting things</u> on his skateboard. tricks

b Justin is Hannah's <u>mother's brother's son</u>. ....

c Hannah waits for her <u>day when she is a year older</u>. ....

d Hannah works well at school and gets good <u>numbers from her teachers</u>. ....

e When Hannah falls off her skateboard, she thinks, 'This is <u>very bad</u>.' ....

f The skateboard and helmet are <u>very good</u> presents. ....

g Evan's questions are <u>not very good</u>, Hannah thinks. ....

WORD WORK 2

These words don't match the pictures. Correct them.

a ~~step~~

...bench...

b parking lot

....

c baby

....

d clap

....

e park

....

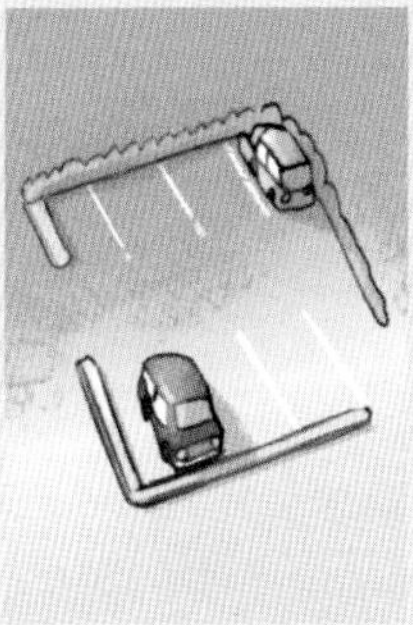

f fall down

....

g bench

....

h grass

....

Complete the sentences with words from Chapters 3 and 4.

a Hannah wants to skateboard a l o n e.

b Hannah needs more _ _ a _ _ i _ e on her skateboard.

c Owen can go up in the _ _ r and come down again.

d Michael's mother says, 'Michael, _ _ y again.'

e The woman on the bicycle says, '_ a _   _ u _ _' when Hannah falls off.

f The office building is two b _ o _ k _ from Hannah's house.

WORD WORK 3

1 Find words from Chapters 5 and 6 in the skateboards to match the pictures.

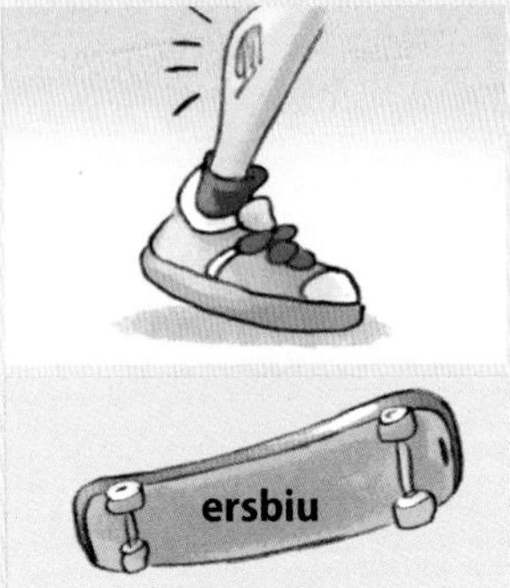

a ......bruise...... **b** .... **c** ....

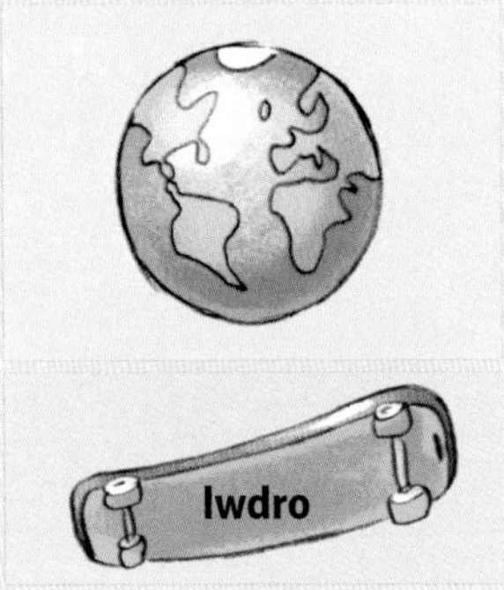

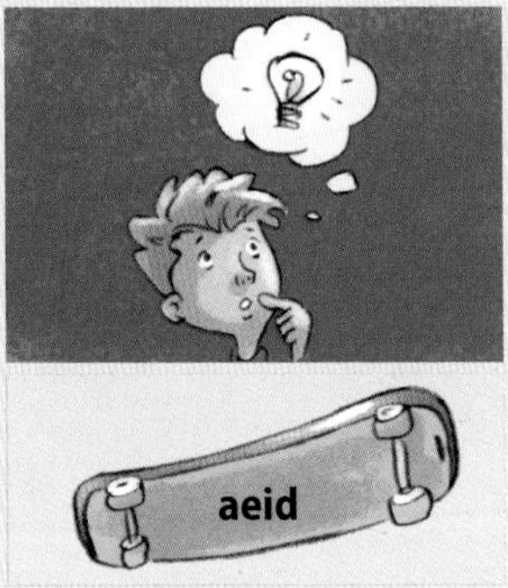

d .... **e** .... **f** ....

2 Complete each sentence with a word from the box.

~~around~~ high real sure tough

a 'Go Skateboarding Day' happens on June 21st all ......around...... the world.

b Very good skateboarders can do .... tricks.

c Hannah can do tricks! She's a .... skateboarder now.

d Owen can jump .... in the air on his skateboard.

e '..................!' answers Hannah when Owen says, 'Everybody falls off sometimes.'

GRAMMAR CHECK

There is and there are

We use there is and there are to talk about things and people in a place.
We use there is (or there's) with a singular noun, and there are with a plural noun.

There's a big present from her mother and father on the table.

There are some people at the skatepark.

Negative forms are there isn't and there aren't.

There isn't a car in the park, and there aren't any bicycles.

Complete the sentences with *there is, there are, there isn't* or *there aren't*.

a Near Hannah's house ...there is... a new skatepark.
b .... some trees near the skatepark.
c .... any girl skateboarders at the skatepark.
d .... a skateboard under Justin's arm. Can you see it?
e .... one skateboarder in the air, and everybody's looking at him.
f At the skatepark, ... any cars.
g .... a smile on Hannah's face when she falls down.
h .... some skateboarders on the walls.
i .... a baby on a skateboard. Don't be dumb!
j .... any flowers at the skatepark.

GRAMMAR CHECK

Possessive adjectives

We use possessive adjectives to say who something belongs to.

Hannah thinks, 'My birthday's coming soon.'

There are possessive adjectives for the different personal pronouns.

singular		**plural**	
I	my	we	our
you	your	you	your
he	his	they	their
she	her		
it	its		

2 Complete the sentences with the words in the box.

Her his Its My Our their Their ~~your~~ your

a 'Evan, ...your...... idea is awesome.'

b 'This helmet is nice. .... colours are awesome, too.'

c '.................. mom really listens to me,' Hannah thinks.

d 'Look at Owen. I love .... skateboarding.'

e 'I'm sorry for Hannah. .... bruises are terrible.'

f 'Watch Owen and his friends. .... tricks are really very good.'

g 'Hey, Hannah, ... new skateboard is awesome!'

h '.................. daughter has very good grades,' Hannah's Mom and Dad think.

i 'Evan and Hannah are with .... cousin Justin,' Hannah's mom says.

GRAMMAR CHECK

Time clauses with before, after, and when

We can put before, after and when clauses at the start of the sentence or at the end. When a time clause goes first in a sentence, we put a comma (,) after it.

Before Hannah goes to school, she does some skateboarding practice.

Hannah does some skateboarding practice before she goes to school.

After Evan comes into the kitchen, his mother goes out.

His mother goes out of the kitchen after Evan comes in.

When Evan goes to work, he goes past the skatepark.

Evan goes past the skatepark when he goes to work.

The linker before links a later action with an earlier action; after links an earlier action with a later action; when links two actions near in time. Often with when, the first action is the reason for the second action.

Complete the sentences with *before, after* and *when*.

a ....When.... Hannah gets on Justin's skateboard, she doesn't stay on it for long.

b .... Hannah's birthday arrives, she talks to her mother and father.

c .... she opens the present from her mother and father, Hannah opens Evan's present to her.

d .... Evan asks dumb questions, Hannah is angry with him.

e Hannah is excited .... she takes her new skateboard to the skatepark.

f Hannah sits down on a bench .... she leaves the skatepark.

g .... Michael falls over, he gets up again.

h .... Hannah tells her mother all about her practice, she says, 'Don't laugh.'

i .... Justin calls his cousin, he tells her about 'Go Skateboarding Day'.

j Everybody stops and watches .... Owen does his trick.

DOMINOES Your Choice

Read *Dominoes* for pleasure, or to develop language skills. It's your choice.

Each *Domino* reader includes:

- a good story to enjoy
- integrated activities to develop reading skills and increase vocabulary
- task-based projects – perfect for CEFR portfolios
- contextualized grammar activities

Each *Domino* pack contains a reader, and an excitingly dramatized audio recording of the story

If you liked this *Domino*, read these:

Lisa's Song

Lesley Thompson

Al Brown plays the guitar in a band with friends. He writes songs, too. 'Our boy can't live without his music,' his parents say.

But when Al's baby sister, Lisa, arrives from hospital, his life is suddenly different. Now his mother and father have no time for him, and he has no time for school work – or the band.

Then Al's sister is ill. And Grandad tells him, 'Write a song for Lisa!' But why, and how can this help?

Pebbles on the Beach

Alex Raynham

Abby is a teenager, and doesn't talk much to her parents. Abby's dad works hard for an oil company, and Abby's mom doesn't like her friends. Then, one summer, she stays with her crazy Aunt May in California. Here – with Aunt May and her young neighbours Diego and Bianca – she learns to see things differently. But, one night, there's an oil spill on the beautiful beach near their home.

What can Abby, her aunt, and the neighbours do? And who answers Abby's call for more help? And how?

	CEFR	Cambridge Exams	IELTS	TOEFL iBT	TOEIC
Level 3	B1	PET	4.0	57-86	550
Level 2	A2–B1	KET-PET	3.0-4.0	–	390
Level 1	A1–A2	YLE Flyers/KET	3.0	–	225
Starter & Quick Starter	A1	YLE Movers	1.0–2.0	–	–

You can find details and a full list of books and teachers' resources on our website:

www.oup.com/elt/gradedreaders